latin dance

Galveston County
System
Galveston Co.. Texas

Isabel Thomas

Lerner Publications Company
Minneapolis

First American edition published in 2012 by Lerner Publishing Group, Inc. Published by arrangement with Wayland, a division of Hachette Children's Books

Lerner Publications Company
A division of Lerner Publishing Group, Inc.
241 First Avenue North
Minneapolis, MN U.S.A.

Website address: www.lernerbooks.com

Library of Congress Cataloging-in-Publication Data

Thomas, Isabel, 1980–
    Latin dance / by Isabel Thomas.
      p.   cm. — (On the radar: dance)
    Includes index.
    ISBN 978-0-7613-7762-7 (lib. bdg. : alk. paper)
    1. Dance—Latin America—Juvenile literature.
I. Title.
GV1596.5.T56 2012
793.3'3—dc22   2011006118

Manufactured in the United States of America
 – CG – 7/15/11

Photo Acknowledgments
Images in this book are used with the permission of: Getty: Ian Gavan/Stringer 8-9; Photolibrary: Age Fotostock 6 tr; Rex Features: SNAP 15; Shutterstock: Akva 14tr, Efanov Aleksey Anatolievich 1, 2cl, 6cl, Anky 16tr, Marcelo Roberto Caba cover, 3br, Dmitry Matrosov 23tr, My New Images 23tl, Damian Palus 22br, Jack Qi 26-27, Simone Simone 16bl, Stepanov 2-3, Aleksandar Todorovic 26cl, Valua Vitaly 23br, Gary Yim 2b, 4-5, 30, 30-31.

Main body text set in
Helvetica Neue LT Std 13/15.5.
Typeface provided by Adobe Systems.

cover stories

the**people**

the**moves**

the**talk**

LATIN DANCE

Flamboyant and passionate, Latin dance is one of the most expressive and energetic dance forms. It has a rich and colorful history.

African influence

In the sixteenth century, many African slaves were brought to the New World. They brought with them their own music and dance that featured new rhythms and beats. These rhythms soon spread throughout North and South America and fused with native dances found there. The result was Latin dance—a variety of dynamic and fast-paced dance styles such as the salsa, the samba, the cha-cha, the rumba, and the tango.

Exotic dances

Many governments and religions were against these new dance styles. For example, the sensuous samba, which was brought by African slaves into Brazil, was seen as a sinful dance by the Europeans.

Dance evolution

Over time, as dance has evolved, new styles have borrowed moves from Latin dances. *Ceroc*, for example, is a fusion of salsa, hip-hop, ballroom, tango, and jive. Television has played a part too. Dance programs have helped to make Latin dance more popular than ever. Long live Latin!

Dance checklist

• Good rhythm and timing
• Strength and stamina—
  some dances are demanding.
• A sensational hip wiggle!
• A sense of style and drama

tango

salsa

rumba

paso doble

THE DANCES

Latin dances are famous for their fast rhythms and intricate footwork. Dancers do not just listen to the music, they feel the rhythms and tell a story with their moves.

cha-cha

Salsa

This sizzling party dance is packed with fast, intricate turns and sassy hip movements. As dancers let their weight settle onto each leg, they push the hips out to the side. The upper body stays straight and level for the ultimate hip wiggle!

Tango

Originating in Argentina, the tango is about the relationship between a man and a woman. It is famous for its slow, powerful steps; staccato movements; passionate holds; and expressive, storytelling gestures.

Rumba

The passionate rumba is famous for its sensual hip action and quick spot turns. Dancers keep the waist loose, letting the hips sway from side to side. Intense eye contact turns the dance into a romantic love story.

Paso doble

Dramatic paso doble dancers step as though they are marching or stamping, holding the head and the chest high. Sharp arm and hand movements tell a story of passion.

Cha-cha

Superfast synchronized moves are the main focus of the cha-cha. Light footwork is a must to keep up with the bubbly rhythms. This dance has a distinctive "step, step, cha, cha, cha" rhythm to follow.

BRIAN FORTUNA

THE STATS
Name: Brian Fortuna
Born: September 20, 1982
Place of birth:
Philadelphia, Pennsylvania
Job: Professional
dancer, choreographer,
and instructor

Brian burns the floor with Ali Bastian!

Early years

Brian has dancing in his genes. Both of his
parents are successful Latin dancers who own a
dance school. They began teaching him to dance
when he was four years old. By his teens, he was so
good that he was following in his parents' footsteps
and teaching dance himself.

Following his dreams

Brian studied business in college but decided to follow his passion for performing. He moved to Los Angeles, California, and landed small TV presenting jobs on *Dancing with the Stars* and *American Idol*. At the same time, he taught dance and choreographed Latin dance teams.

On the big screen

Brian's reputation as a great dance teacher soon won him work in Hollywood. He choreographed and danced in the TV drama *South Beach* and was featured as a dancer in the film *The Aviator* (2004), which starred Leonardo DiCaprio.

Making it big

In 2007 Brian joined the hit show *Dancing with the Stars* and was partnered with former Miss USA Shandi Finnessey. The following year, he appeared in the British version, *Strictly Come Dancing,* for the first time. In 2009 he partnered with popular British soap star Ali Bastian on *Strictly*. Brian's choreography and skills helped them to achieve high scores throughout the competition.

Dance passion

Brian is passionate about getting people dancing. In 2010 he choreographed the TV show *Dancing on Wheels*, featuring wheelchair ballroom and Latin dance. In the same year, he turned up the heat onstage with Ali Bastian in the popular stage production of *Burn the Floor*. When it comes to Latin dance, Brian scores a perfect 10!

Career highlights

2003 won the North American Amateur Latin Championships

2004 starred in the Canadian documentary *Live to Dance*

2007 performed at the Oscars and won the Christmas special of *Strictly Come Dancing*

2010 released *Latin Jam*, a collection of music for street salsa—his favorite dance

2011 earned a WhatsOnStage.com award nomination for London Newcomer of the Year for his performance in *Burn the Floor*

LOVING LATIN!

Harriet Bell's story

I was fourteen years old when I began ballroom and Latin dancing. One of my best friends had danced in a national competition, and it sounded so glamorous. I'd done other styles of dancing, but just hearing about Latin made me want to do it! At my first dance class, I fell totally in love with Latin's energy and rhythm.

I soon discovered that Latin dance is really social, and I made a lot of new friends. Once we'd mastered the basics, a group of us entered our first competition. I was so proud when my partner and I got through to the final round and won second place for our cha-cha! The fun of competitions isn't just about you dancing. It's about watching other dancers' styles and picking up tips to improve your own.

After the competition, I stepped up my class and practice time to fifteen hours a week, including helping out in the beginners' classes. My dancing improved quickly, and I began to compete at the national level. I love taking part in shows and contests. The whole floor suddenly comes alive, and all you can see is a whirl of gorgeous, colorful dresses and people smiling and having fun!

These days, dancing takes up a lot of my time, but I will never for a moment regret starting Latin dance. I love to watch reality TV dance shows and dream that one day I will be as good as some of the professional dancers. I definitely think I'm at my happiest when I dance. I usually have an enormous grin on my face. Latin is so special, and nothing can take that away from me.

BASIC SALSA

Salsa is an energetic party dance that is lots of fun! The movement is mainly in the hips and the legs. This basic salsa move is a rocking step, forward and backward.

You will need:

- space to dance
- a dance partner
- salsa music

F Hold your partner's hands. Step backward with your right foot, and put your weight onto it.

M Hold your partner's hands. Step forward with your left foot, and put your weight onto it.

Note: To indicate the gender differences in the step-by-step spreads, **F** refers to a female dancer's steps and **M** to a male dancer's steps.

F Step forward with your right foot, bend your left knee, and lift your left foot off the floor.

M Step back with your left foot. Bend your right leg. Lift your right foot off the floor.

3

F Step forward with your left foot, and rock forward on it.

M Step back with your right foot, rocking backward on it.

4

F Bring your right leg forward to join your left leg. Bend your right knee. Start again with step 1.

M Bring your left leg back to join your right leg, bending your left knee. Start again with step 1.

Got it?

Fluid salsa moves involve transferring the weight from one leg to the other. This movement, in turn, moves the hips. It is important to follow the rhythm of salsa music when you are doing these steps.

13

COME DANCING!

From school gym lessons to prime-time Saturday night TV, Latin dance fever is enjoying a popularity explosion! So how did sassy samba, salsa, and tango moves become such a big hit?

Seen it in the movies

The "Latin boom" in America in the 1930s and 1940s created a range of new musical styles. Hollywood films of the time helped to bring the style, poise, and glamour of Latin dance to a worldwide audience. For example, *Rumba* (1935) showcased popular Latin dance styles. The 1980s saw a surge in Latin dance popularity, helping to make the 1987 film *Dirty Dancing* become a massive box-office success and one of the best-loved movies of all time.

On the small screen

Successful Latin American singers such as Ricky Martin and Shakira helped to bring Latin music and dance to a wider audience during the 1990s.

In the early 2000s, the trend for celebrity TV contests and reality shows led to a dance-based version called *Dancing with the Stars*. It pairs professional dancers with celebrities in a ballroom and Latin dance tournament. The show has given Latin dance superstar status and has encouraged increasing numbers of viewers to take it up for themselves.

Another reality show, *So You Think You Can Dance*, takes its cue from the popular *American Idol*. Contestants audition in major U.S. cities for a chance to perform in a variety of styles, including Latin, for prizes or cash.

The love story

The theater has not escaped the Latin dance bug, either. Twenty years after the movie *Dirty Dancing* opened, the stage version became a worldwide hit, from London's West End to Broadway!

The Latin success story shows no sign of ending soon. From TV to theater and dance classes, the public's love affair with Latin dance is still going strong. These dances are sassy and hot—and they are heading to a ballroom near you!

The slick Latin dance routines of *Dirty Dancing* turned its stars Jennifer Grey and Patrick Swayze into dance-film legends.

LATIN LANGUAGE

Here's a quick and easy guide to the Latin lingo in this book.

bateria
a percussion band that plays samba music

batucada
a type of extremely fast-moving samba

Carnival
a festival held just before the start of the Christian period of Lent

ceroc
a popular type of dance that mixes Latin with hip-hop and jive

choreographer
a dance teacher who puts moves to music to create dance routines

flamenco
a style of dancing that originated in Spain. It is very rhythmic and involves dramatic hand claps and foot stamps.

jive
a lively dance that originated in the United States in the 1940s. It involves fast-paced leg kicks, flicks, and spins.

matador
the Spanish word for a bullfighter

passistas
the male dancers in the Rio de Janeiro Carnival in Brazil

promenades
the powerful, striding steps used when dancing the tango

sambadrome
the parade ground in which samba is danced during the Rio de Janeiro Carnival

sashay
dancing and gliding in a diagonal or sideways manner

shimmy
a dance move in which the dancer shakes the hips and shoulders

spot turn
a turn used to change direction when dancing the rumba

surdo drum
a large drum played by a samba drummer

matador

GLOSSARY

adrenaline
a hormone found in the body that causes the heart to beat faster and gives the dancer a "rushing" feeling

beading
tiny beads that are sewn into fabric to add decoration or detail

bodice
a piece of clothing that fits firmly around the chest and the waist

fused
joined or combined

hip-hop
a style of music and dance that originated in the 1970s in the United States

intricate
very detailed and complex

perfectionist
a person who wants to meet the highest standards in anything he or she does

plumes
large, showy feathers often used on headdresses or costumes

sensuous
passionate and expressive

spangles
small, sparkling objects (such as sequins) that are sewn onto costumes for decoration

staccato
in music, a word for short, separate notes or movements

stamina
great physical or mental strength that allows you to do something for a long time

synchronize
when dancers coordinate their movements in time to music

SIMPLE TANGO

If you like drama, you will love the tango. This dance features close body contact, promenade steps, and staccato head movements.

You will need:

- space to dance
- a dance partner
- tango music

1

F Turn your head to look away from your partner. Place your left hand on your partner's right shoulder.

M Hold your partner's right hand out to the side. Look toward your left hand. Place your right hand on your partner's back.

2

F Step backward onto your right foot.

M Step quickly forward onto your left foot, keeping your right leg stretched behind you.

3

F Step backward onto your left foot.

M Step forward quickly onto your right foot.

4

F Step quickly backward onto your right foot.

M Step forward quickly onto your left foot.

5

F Mirror your partner's move with your right leg. Then flick your head forward.

M Slide your right leg forward to join your left leg. Slide your left leg out to the side.

Got it?

The tango is a dramatic "striding" dance, which should be strong and proud to reflect the beat of the music. Steps 1 to 4 are a series of strong, driving steps in which the couple travels across the floor. Step 5 is a finishing flourish to the dance.

A WEEK IN THE LIFE OF LATIN DANCE COMPETITOR

MATT TWEEDALE

blog   news   events

Monday

It's the first day of my dancing week, and I helped to teach the beginners' Latin and ballroom classes at the university. Teaching really helps me to perfect my own dance technique because I get to practice the simple steps that are a core part of our team's routines.

Tuesday

I worked on my fitness and stamina this morning, with an hour in the gym followed by an hour of swimming. Our dance class was amazing this evening! We developed a flashy new salsa routine, then finished the night with some jive dancing to Christina Aguilera's "Candyman." It was great fun, and it helped us all to relax.

Wednesday

No gym today. I wanted to give my body time to recover. Instead, I had a leisurely breakfast—yogurt, granola, and fruit—before my training session with the dance team to prepare for Saturday's national dance competition. My partner, Ruth, and I ran through our

blog   news   events

cha-cha about ten times! After all that practice, I know our footwork is going to be perfect!

Friday

I spent the morning packing for the competition. We take lots of luggage to competitions because we need our competition outfits as well as everyday clothes. The girls have even more bags because of their hairstyling gear, accessories, and makeup! In the afternoon, we set off for the hotel where we were staying for the event.

Saturday

Competition day! Around 900 couples were taking part in the whole event. The atmosphere was tense, and everyone was so excited. The Latin section was in the afternoon. Ruth and I were couple number 137, and we were thrilled to get through to the quarterfinals with our cha-cha and jive routines. This put us in the top 32 couples out of the 600 contestants taking part in the Latin section!

After the Latin section, our dance team took part in the team competition and won—making us Division A champions! We left the ballroom at 11:30 p.m., happy and tired—but with enough energy for one more dance to celebrate our success!

TOTAL GLAMOUR

Latin costumes are designed to dazzle, with sparkling sequins, jewels, and tassles; with coordinating colors; and a body-hugging fit. But they must also let the dancers move their arms, legs, and hips easily.

For the men

The man's outfit is modeled on a traditional suit: black dance trousers with a white or black shirt or a stretchy fitted top. There may be a touch of glitzy decoration, fringing, or flashes of color to tie in with his partner's costume.

Stunning samba headdresses add to the glamour of Carnival!

Accessorize

The most famous Latin dance accessories are the flamboyant headdresses worn by Brazilian samba dancers at Carnival time. This glamorous headwear can include huge plumes, birds, fruit, or flowers, and sparkling satin, beads, or sequins—all in an explosion of colors!

Longer legs

Women's dance shoes are usually heeled to lengthen the legs. This can make dancing difficult, so training sessions in heeled shoes are necessary to be able to dance comfortably!

Spangled or sequined dance shoes have ankle straps to help them stay on.

Latin ladies

For women dancers, a glamorous glittery or floaty dress is essential. A fitted, low-backed bodice helps the dancer move freely, while a swishy, flowing skirt flicks out with every wiggle of the hip. Crystals and beading are designed to shimmer and catch the light.

Fancy footwear

For men, dancing shoes with flexible leather soles slide smoothly across the floor without skidding and allow the foot to "feel" the floor.

Dramatic makeup can help to create a dance "character."

Fake it!

The audience and judges see dancers from a distance and usually under bright lights. Bold makeup helps to emphasize the dancers' features and adds to the drama of the dance. Women also often wear fake nails, eyelashes, and a fake tan to spice up their look.

SUSANA MONTERO

Susana is a top Latin dance choreographer and winner of the British Salsa Dance Championships. She has worked on star-studded shows such as *So You Think You Can Dance?* and *Strictly Come Dancing.* On the Radar asks her the questions *you* want to know.

Why do you think Latin dance classes are so popular?

Latin dance has the feel-good factor! You can relax at a Latin dance class and really come out of your shell. Latin is such a social dance too. It's a great excuse to forget your troubles and just have fun!

What is so thrilling about Latin dance?

Latin is the most passionate and emotional dance form. You feel an intense connection with your partner, and this makes it such a beautiful dance to watch.

What's been your big career highlight so far?

Doing the choreography for *So You Think You Can Dance?* The competitors are so talented, professional, and easy to work with. I hope watching this show inspires more people to express themselves through dance.

What is it like to work on Britain's *Strictly Come Dancing?*

Amazing! The atmosphere is electric, and it's fantastic to watch the celebrities develop their skills and techniques. I love working on the show and contributing to the choreography—it's wonderful to see your very own ideas put into action!

How can On the Radar readers pursue a career in Latin dance?

It takes passion, determination, and time. You have to be a perfectionist and practice every step over and over. If dancing is your passion, you'll have the drive to push yourself and improve your dancing to competition level.

24

Do you have to be good at other types of dancing?

Not at all—Latin is a great dance for beginners. As long as you love to dance, you can Latin dance!

Did you start Latin dancing as a child?

No—from the age of five, I had a passion for ballet and flamenco and learned both of these. I was introduced to salsa as an adult. The style of the dance totally gripped me, and I haven't looked back!

Do you need a partner to start?

No partner needed! You can get started with salsa, samba, and several other styles on your own or in a group, with everyone dancing solo.

25

THE PASO DOBLE

The paso doble is inspired by the drama and danger of a Spanish bullfight and is performed to a marchlike beat. It is always danced in pairs. The male and the female play different roles to bring this impressive dance to life!

The bullfighter

The male dancer takes the role of the bullfighter, or matador. Quick, dramatic movements show his pride and courage when he enters the ring. His chin is lowered as he watches the bull carefully. Strong arm lines, posture, and powerful foot stamps show his confidence in the face of danger.

The swirling cape

The female dancer plays the role of the bullfighter's cape, spinning around the ring with long, sweeping steps. She may also act as the bull. Her chin tilts upward to create elegant lines. Her dress is long and flows like a cape. Bold colors, such as black or deep red, add to the drama of the dance.

Strike a pose

Paso doble music features several breaks, or "crashes." Routines are carefully choreographed to allow the dancers to strike dramatic poses at each break. The dance becomes more and more exciting as the battle between the bull and the bullfighter comes to an end.

EASY RUMBA

The rumba is a super-slow dance also known as "the dance of love." The emphasis is on smooth, flowing body and hip movements rather than on detailed footwork.

You will need:

- space to dance
- a dance partner
- rumba music

1

(M) Hold your partner's right hand away from her body at shoulder height. Your right hand should be placed on her back. Step forward with your left foot toward her right leg.

(F) Place your left hand on your partner's right shoulder. Step backward with your right foot.

2

(M) Step backward with your right foot.

(F) Step forward with your left foot.

3

| M | Slide your left leg to the side. |
| F | Slide your right leg to the side. |

| M | Slide your right leg in front of your left, bringing your body with you. Extend your right arm out as your partner extends her left arm. |
| F | Slide your left leg in front of your right, bringing your body with you. Extend your right arm out as your partner extends his left arm. |

4

Got it?

You should have maintained the same hold throughout steps 1 to 3 before releasing the hold in step 4. Your movements should have been perfectly synchronized.

CARNIVAL!

It's the climax of the Rio de Janeiro Carnival in Brazil. As your samba club's spectacular float waits near the sambadrome, you hear the roar of the crowd. Inside are 100,000 people, all waiting to see you dance. Your body tingles with nervous energy, and your mind races through the samba routines that you've practiced throughout the year.

Sparkling sashay

Fireworks erupt like brilliant flowers of fire in the sky, signaling that it's time for your bateria to parade. Your heart beats faster. Every inch of your body sparkles with makeup, spangles, and crystals. Huge colorful plumes sway above your head and cascade down to the floor. Despite the weight of your costume and the heat of the Brazilian night, you feel amazing.

The world is watching

Multicolored costumes gleam like rare jewels, and headdresses shimmer and shake as you move in perfect timing with the passistas around you. It seems as though the whole country has stopped to watch the parade. Tonight, the sambadrome is the center of your world.

Explosive energy

The atmosphere is electric as you dance at the world's biggest party. The driving pace of the surdo drums is so loud you can feel the beat in your bones. Huge decorated floats parade down the arena, and hundreds of drummers bang out batucada rhythms, urging you to swing, shimmy, and sashay to the beat of the music.

The party's hardly started!

You've been dancing for more than an hour, but it feels like five minutes. An adrenaline rush carries everyone out of the stadium to continue the party on the streets. The heat wraps around you like a blanket, but the carnival is just getting started. Party on!

GET MORE INFO

Books & DVDs

Durango, Julia. *Under the Mambo Moon*. Watertown, MA: Charlesbridge Publishing, 2011. Poetry describes popular forms of Latin dance in this illustrated book.

Hamilton, S. L. *Latin*. Edina, MN: Abdo Publishing Company, 2011. Latin dance moves are profiled in this Xtreme Dance title.

Levy, Elizabeth. *Seventh-Grade Tango*. New York: Hyperion, 2001. Follow the progress of two teen dance partners in this novel about the tangle of growing up while learning the tango.

Websites

Crazy for Salsa
http://www.salsacrazy.com/dance-blog.html
This website pulls together information about Latin dance events around the United States and the world and offers many dance videos on the various styles of Latin dance.

International DanceSport Federation
http://www.worlddancesport.org/About/Dance%20Styles/Latin+%26+Standard
This site has general information about DanceSport as well as videos of the most recent international Latin dance championships.

USA Dance
http://www.usadance.org/
The mission of this nonprofit website is to promote Latin dancing across the United States in elementary, middle, and high schools. The group also supports efforts to make ballroom dancing—called DanceSport—an Olympic sport.

INDEX